THE HIDDEN SECRETS OF WEALTH & ABUNDANCE

CONTENTS

Introduction

Chapter 1: The Foundation of Wealth Alchemy

Chapter 2: The Power of Ancient Words for Wealth

Chapter 3: Daily Wealth Alignment Routine

Chapter 4: Weekly Wealth Rituals and Practices

Chapter 5: Word-Spells and Ancient Incantations for Wealth

Chapter 6: Monthly and Seasonal Wealth Rituals

Chapter 7: Alchemical Practices for Inner Wealth

Chapter 8: Creating a Personalized Wealth Path

Final Thoughts

INTRODUCTION

Welcome, seeker of wealth and wisdom. You can call me "Spooky"—a fitting pseudonym, perhaps, for someone who delves into the hidden, the mystical, and the unseen.

I remain anonymous not to create distance, but to remove the distractions of identity, allowing the knowledge within this book to speak for itself. Who I am matters less than what I have to share, and that is the alchemy of wealth.

For centuries, secret societies, ancient philosophers, and brilliant minds have guarded knowledge that bridges the spiritual and material worlds, promising transformation to those who understand it.

Nikola Tesla, Leonardo da Vinci, Isaac Newton, and others were rumored to have tapped into these very principles, understanding that the universe is energy, and that the mind is both a powerful receiver and transmitter of it. Their works inspired new ideas, inventions, and ways of thinking that redefined the world.

This book distills that knowledge, drawn from the teachings of alchemists, hermetic philosophers, and those who harnessed unseen forces to achieve greatness. Yet unlike some teachings that rely on positive thinking alone or surface-level advice, this is deeper, older, and perhaps a bit... spooky.

WHY I'M SHARING THIS

In times when wealth is more fluid than ever, understanding how to align ourselves with prosperity isn't just valuable—it's essential. I've seen, felt, and experienced the transformative power of these teachings, and I believe they belong to those ready to receive them.

Whether you're starting from scratch or seeking a new dimension in your financial life, this book will guide you step by step into the ancient art of wealth alchemy.

THE SOURCE OF THIS KNOWLEDGE

The practices you'll find here are inspired by the works of mystical figures like Hermes Trismegistus, the Emerald Tablet, and various alchemical texts.

They're fused with contemporary understandings of energy, vibration, and psychological alignment, adapted to help you attract and sustain the wealth you desire.

Each chapter combines historical insights with practical techniques, so you can incorporate these teachings into your life today.

Let the pages that follow serve as your guide to wealth—not just in the material sense, but in spirit, mind, and purpose. As you begin, know that this path is one of transformation.

To those prepared to embrace it, I welcome you to the journey.

BACKSTORY AND ORIGINS OF THE KNOWLEDGE

The roots of wealth alchemy are deeply interwoven with ancient mystical traditions, from Egyptian Hermeticism to the alchemical sciences of the Renaissance, and the esoteric practices of Kabbalah.

Unlike contemporary teachings that present wealth as a simple product of positive thinking, these ancient traditions view prosperity as a sophisticated interplay of thought, energy, ritual, and alignment with natural forces.

This book draws from these arcane sources, synthesising teachings from texts like the *Tabula Smaragdina* (Emerald Tablet), Hermeticism, and even early ceremonial magic.

Many of these concepts, long held as secrets by mystical societies, were guarded due to their complexity and transformative potential. Unlike popular Law of Attraction teachings that focus on mental visualisation, these ancient practices involve a disciplined approach that combines intention with symbolic action, rituals, and personal transformation. Here, we take a deep dive into wealth as energy and align with it using practices that encompass mind, body, and spirit.

WHY MODERN LAW OF ATTRACTION BOOKS FALL SHORT

While the Law of Attraction has popularised the idea that "thoughts become things," it often oversimplifies the process, leading people to feel frustrated or disillusioned when desired results don't materialise.

This is because pure thought alone rarely brings about tangible change. In most traditional practices, the mind is only the starting point; it must be followed by aligned actions, rituals, and, most importantly, a release of limiting beliefs.

Many modern teachings also overlook the importance of personal energy and internal transformation. Simply visualising wealth while carrying hidden fears or doubts about money results in an internal conflict that often blocks the very prosperity we seek.

Ancient wealth practices focus on clearing these internal barriers first, followed by ritualised steps to ground intentions in the physical world.

CORE PRINCIPLES OF WEALTH ALCHEMY

This book is based on principles that ancient mystics and alchemists held as vital truths. Here are the foundational concepts:

1. **All Is Mind (Mentalism)**: This Hermetic principle teaches that reality is fundamentally mental, meaning our thoughts shape our experience. Wealth alchemy begins with transforming the mind to align with prosperity.
2. **As Above, So Below (Correspondence)**: This principle suggests that the microcosm reflects the macrocosm. Our internal beliefs and external actions must align for wealth to flow freely.
3. **Vibration and Resonance**: Everything has a vibrational frequency, including money. By raising our own frequency through specific words, actions, and rituals, we can "tune in" to the energy of abundance.
4. **Energy of Release and Gathering**: Alchemists believed that creation requires both release and accumulation. For wealth, this means letting go of scarcity-based beliefs while simultaneously attracting prosperity through focused intention and ritual.
5. **The Role of Symbols and Rituals**: Unlike modern teachings that rely solely on the mind, ancient practices use symbols, candles, herbs, and spoken words to anchor intention and create alignment with specific outcomes.

BOOK OUTLINE AND CHAPTER PROGRESSION

With these principles established, we can now proceed into practical routines and structured practices that build wealth alignment on every level—mental, energetic, and physical.

CHAPTER 1: THE FOUNDATION OF WEALTH ALCHEMY

BEYOND CONVENTIONAL LAW OF ATTRACTION

In our modern world, countless books and teachings proclaim that wealth can be achieved through the power of positive thinking, visualisation, and what's commonly known as the Law of Attraction. While these approaches have popularised the idea that "thoughts become things," many who attempt to use them find themselves frustrated, as simply visualising wealth often fails to bring real results. This chapter explains why typical Law of Attraction teachings often fall short and introduces the deeper principles of wealth alchemy—an approach that combines mental, energetic, and physical alignment to draw in prosperity.

WHY LAW OF ATTRACTION ALONE OFTEN FAILS

Most Law of Attraction teachings focus solely on mental visualisation, which is only the first step. While thoughts are powerful, they must be supported by action, energy alignment, and, perhaps most importantly, the release of limiting beliefs that keep wealth at a distance. Visualising wealth while holding subconscious fears or doubts about money creates an internal conflict that can repel the very prosperity we seek. Wealth alchemy is a comprehensive process that combines intention, symbolic action, and inner transformation, creating a powerful synergy that draws wealth naturally and sustainably.

CORE PRINCIPLES OF WEALTH ALCHEMY

The teachings in this book are rooted in ancient principles that were carefully preserved by mystical societies and alchemists. Here are the five core principles that underlie all wealth alchemy practices, forming the foundation for the routines, rituals, and spells that will follow.

1. Mentalism: All Is Mind

The Hermetic principle of Mentalism teaches that reality is fundamentally mental; everything begins in the mind. In wealth alchemy, this means that our beliefs, thoughts, and attitudes about wealth create a mental framework that shapes our external financial reality. If we think of ourselves as capable and deserving of wealth, we naturally attract opportunities. Conversely, if we hold limiting beliefs about money, we create barriers that keep it at a distance.

Application:

Start by becoming deeply aware of your thoughts about wealth. Reflect on any doubts, fears, or limiting beliefs you have around money. Perhaps you believe that wealth is only for a select few or that it's hard to come by. Identifying these thoughts allows you to begin transforming them, replacing negative thoughts with affirmations like "I am a magnet for prosperity" or "Money flows to me easily." Repeating these affirmations daily reshapes your mental foundation, aligning it with abundance.

2. Correspondence: As Above, So Below

The principle of Correspondence means that patterns exist on every level of reality, from the smallest atom to the vast cosmos. In the context of wealth, this principle teaches us that what we experience externally mirrors our internal world. Our beliefs, emotions, and subconscious attitudes about wealth are reflected in our financial reality.

Application:

Take steps to harmonise your internal beliefs and external actions with wealth. Start by transforming your physical space to reflect abundance. For example, keep your living or workspace clean and organised, free from clutter. Place symbols of wealth—like a crystal, gold item, or image of something you desire financially—where you can see it daily. This creates alignment between your intention for wealth and the space around you, enhancing your wealth magnetism.

3. Vibration and Resonance: Aligning with Wealth Frequency

The concept of vibration suggests that everything in the universe, including wealth, has a frequency. When we focus on wealth with positive energy, we begin to resonate at the same frequency as prosperity. This is the underlying principle of attraction, which is amplified through rituals, words, and actions that elevate our vibration.

Application:

Raising your vibration to align with wealth involves more than just thinking positively. Specific rituals, like chanting wealth phrases, visualising wealth flowing to you, or using tools like crystals, can help shift your energetic frequency. For example, you might use a phrase like "Lux Fortunae" (meaning "Light of Fortune") to invite wealth energy, repeating it rhythmically to build vibrational resonance.

4. The Energy of Release and Gathering

In alchemy, creation is a process of both release and gathering. For wealth alchemy, this means letting go of scarcity-based thoughts and energy while simultaneously drawing prosperity toward you. Holding onto fears around money blocks the flow of abundance, so releasing these fears becomes essential.

Application:

Practice a daily release ritual. At the end of each day, take a moment to acknowledge and release any financial worries or doubts that arose. Visualise these fears dissolving as you exhale, creating space for wealth energy to gather. Then, visualise wealth flowing into your life with each inhale, reinforcing your openness to receive.

5. The Role of Symbols and Rituals

Ancient practices recognise that the mind alone is not enough to bring change. Physical actions and symbols help anchor intentions, turning abstract thoughts into something tangible. Candles, crystals, specific herbs, and spoken words each carry unique vibrations that contribute to wealth attraction.

Application:

Use tools like a green candle (representing growth and wealth) or a crystal like citrine or pyrite (associated with financial success) during rituals. Lighting a candle, placing a crystal in your workspace, or repeating a wealth mantra creates a ritual that strengthens your alignment with abundance.

INNER TRANSFORMATION IN WEALTH ALCHEMY

Unlike traditional teachings that focus on wealth as an external goal, wealth alchemy sees financial abundance as an extension of personal transformation. By refining ourselves—our thoughts, beliefs, and habits—we become more aligned with prosperity. This process is similar to the alchemical transformation of base metals into gold; we transform limiting aspects of ourselves (doubt, fear, scarcity) into qualities that attract wealth (confidence, trust, abundance).

IDENTIFYING LIMITING BELIEFS

Identifying and releasing limiting beliefs is essential in wealth alchemy. These beliefs often stem from early life experiences or cultural conditioning and may include ideas like "I am not good with money" or "Wealth is for others, not for me." To begin transforming these beliefs, ask yourself what thoughts come to mind when you consider wealth, and note any negative associations or fears that arise.

Transformational Exercise:

- Wealth Transmutation Journal: Start a journal dedicated to identifying and transforming limiting beliefs about wealth. Each time a doubt or fear arises, write it down. Then, write a positive affirmation that directly counters this belief. For instance, replace "Money is hard to come by" with "Money flows to me easily." Over time, this journaling practice will help reshape your internal narrative about wealth.

TOOLS OF WEALTH ALCHEMY

In wealth alchemy, physical tools serve as focal points for intention, helping to amplify the energy directed toward wealth creation. Below are some of the primary tools used in wealth alchemy, along with instructions for incorporating them into your daily practice.

1. Crystals for Wealth

- Citrine: Known as the "merchant's stone," citrine is associated with prosperity and success. Place a citrine crystal in your workspace, carry it with you, or hold it during wealth rituals.
- Pyrite: Often called "fool's gold," pyrite is connected to financial luck and protection. Keep it on your desk or in your wealth area to invite good fortune.

How to Use: During your wealth visualisation exercises, hold the crystal in your hand, imagining it radiating energy that attracts wealth. Alternatively, place it in a space where you handle finances or set intentions for money.

2. Candles for Wealth

- Green Candles: Green symbolises growth, prosperity, and wealth. Lighting a green candle during a ritual invites financial expansion.
- Gold Candles: Gold represents both material wealth and the completion of goals. Use gold candles in high-intensity wealth rituals to reinforce success.

How to Use: Before lighting a candle, state your intention for wealth. Let the candle burn for a short time each day, focusing on your financial goals as the flame burns, symbolising the "burning away" of obstacles to wealth.

3. Herbs and Incense for Wealth

- Basil: Associated with prosperity and wealth protection. Use fresh basil in wealth rituals, add it to a prosperity bath, or carry it in a small sachet as a charm.

- Cinnamon: Known for its fast-acting properties, cinnamon is commonly used to attract wealth quickly. Sprinkle cinnamon powder near a wealth symbol or candle, or carry a small stick in your wallet.

How to Use: Incorporate these herbs into wealth rituals. For example, place basil leaves around your workspace or burn cinnamon incense during wealth meditations.

4. Coins and Symbols of Wealth

- Coins: A direct representation of money. Use a specific coin as a talisman by holding it during wealth rituals or keeping it in a wealth-attracting space.
- Gold or Silver Objects: Place a small gold or silver item on your wealth altar to symbolise enduring prosperity.

How to Use: Coins can be used in various rituals as symbols of wealth, such as the "Prosperous Path" ritual, where coins represent the ongoing accumulation of wealth.

DAILY WEALTH ALIGNMENT PRACTICE

With these foundational principles and tools in place, you can now incorporate them into a daily wealth alignment routine. This practice combines visualisation, energy alignment, and physical tools to reinforce your intentions for prosperity.

1. Morning Affirmation: Upon waking, affirm "I am open to wealth; I am aligned with prosperity." Repeat this three times to start your day with intention.
2. Wealth Visualisation: Close your eyes and imagine wealth as a glowing golden light that surrounds you. See it filling you with warmth and attracting prosperity.

3. Setting Up Symbols: Place a small symbol of wealth (such as a coin, crystal, or basil leaf) where you'll see it often. Let this remind you of your alignment with wealth throughout the day.
4. Evening Reflection: Before bed, review any limiting beliefs or thoughts that arose. Write them in your journal, replace them with affirmations, and express gratitude for the wealth that's already in your life.

This foundational chapter lays the groundwork for your journey in wealth alchemy. By embracing these principles, transforming limiting beliefs, and incorporating powerful symbols, you prepare yourself to attract and sustain financial abundance. With this foundation, you're now ready to explore practical routines, spells, and rituals that deepen your connection to wealth and align you with the frequency of abundance.

CHAPTER 2: THE POWER OF ANCIENT WORDS

WORDS AS ENERGY AND VIBRATION

In many ancient traditions, words and sounds are considered more than simple expressions; they're understood as tools of creation with the power to shape reality. This concept can be found across mystical and spiritual traditions—from the Hermetic idea that "all is vibration" to the Vedic mantras of Hinduism, where specific sounds are said to align the speaker with universal forces.

The wealth-oriented words and phrases in this chapter are not just affirmations but are considered "word-spells" or "vibrational keys" that align your energy with prosperity. Each one has been selected for its traditional association with wealth and is intended to serve as a focal point for your intentions. When spoken or chanted, these words are thought to tune your personal frequency to the energy of abundance.

THE SCIENCE OF SOUND AND WORDS

The impact of sound on the material world has been studied through cymatics, where specific frequencies create structured patterns in matter (such as sand on a vibrating plate). These studies suggest that sound has a measurable effect on physical reality, supporting ancient ideas that words and sounds can shape energy.

In wealth alchemy, using sound in the form of spoken words allows us to engage both the mind and body in setting intentions. By chanting, affirming, or repeating a specific word or phrase, we create a resonance that aligns us with the energy of prosperity. Unlike silent visualisation, speaking a wealth word adds depth to your intention, allowing it to become a full-body experience.

Ancient Wealth Words and Their Meanings

Below are several ancient words and phrases specifically associated with wealth, prosperity, and attraction. Each entry explains the origin, meaning, and method for using the word or phrase in wealth practices.

1. Abracadabra

Meaning: "I create as I speak." Derived from ancient Aramaic, this word is traditionally used as a word of power, believed to bring thoughts and desires into physical form through spoken intention. Abracadabra has appeared in texts from various cultures, where it is used as both a protective word and a creative phrase.

How to Use:

- **Daily Wealth Chant**: Write down your financial goal or intention, such as "I attract $10,000 easily." Hold this paper in your hands while closing your eyes, visualising your goal as a reality.
- Begin chanting "Abracadabra" in a slow, focused tone. Say the word with intention, feeling its resonance in your body. As you repeat it, imagine your intention taking form, building energy with each repetition.
- **Repetition**: Speak "Abracadabra" 9 times, with increasing confidence each time. Finish by saying, "As I speak it, so it becomes," and visualise the energy of the word moving into your goal.

2. Lux Fortunae (Light of Fortune)

Meaning: Latin for "Light of Fortune," this phrase is used to invite luck, wealth, and financial blessings. In the context of wealth alchemy, "Lux Fortunae" is thought to help one "shine" with a light that attracts prosperity and good fortune.

How to Use:

- **Candle Ritual**: Light a green or gold candle, which represents wealth and fortune. Place your hands over your heart, close your eyes, and chant, "Lux Fortunae, Lux Fortunae, Lux Fortunae—light of fortune, shine upon me."
- As you chant, visualise a warm, golden light expanding from your chest, filling your body with prosperity energy and radiating outward. Imagine this light drawing in wealth, success, and opportunities.
- **Repetition**: Chant "Lux Fortunae" 9 times, feeling the warmth of fortune as it fills you. End with, "I am a beacon of fortune and wealth," sealing your intention.

3. Venite Divitiae (Come, Riches)

Meaning: This Latin phrase translates directly to "Come, riches." It is a straightforward and powerful call to financial abundance, inviting wealth into your life.

How to Use:

- **Simple Daily Invocation**: Write "Venite Divitiae" on a small piece of paper and place it under a green candle. Light the candle and visualise wealth flowing to you.

- Chant "Venite Divitiae" 12 times, with each repetition seeing wealth and abundance come closer. Imagine money, success, and resources gathering around you.
- After chanting, say, "By these words, wealth is drawn to me. My life is filled with riches and success." Allow the candle to burn down if possible, keeping the paper with you as a charm.

4. Solvo et Colligo (I Release and I Gather)

Meaning: Latin for "I release and I gather," this phrase embodies the concept of letting go of scarcity-based thoughts and inviting prosperity. In wealth alchemy, it represents both the release of limitations and the gathering of abundance.

How to Use:

- **Rhythmic Chanting**: Sit comfortably, close your eyes, and begin by repeating "Solvo" on each exhale. Imagine all financial fears, doubts, or limiting beliefs dissolving as you release them.
- With each inhale, say "Colligo," visualising wealth, abundance, and opportunities gathering around you.
- **Repetition**: Continue chanting "Solvo et Colligo" for about 5 minutes in a rhythm, alternating between release and gathering. Conclude with "With these words, I release all lack and gather endless wealth."

5. Creare Abundantiam (Create Abundance)

Meaning: "Create abundance" in Latin, this phrase is a direct invocation for generating and attracting wealth and prosperity.

How to Use:

- **Visualisation with Mantra**: Light a green or gold candle, and place a small bowl of coins or crystals in front of you. Visualise the coins multiplying, representing the increase of wealth in your life.
- Chant "Creare Abundantiam" as you visualise. With each repetition, imagine more wealth flowing toward you, multiplying like the coins.
- **Repetition**: Repeat the phrase 9 times, closing with "My abundance is created and flows freely." Keep the bowl in a place of prominence to represent your intention.

USING WORD-SPELLS IN DAILY WEALTH PRACTICES

Incorporating these word-spells into your daily routine creates a consistent alignment with wealth energy. Here are some tips on making them a regular part of your day:

1. **Set a Daily Time for Word-Spells**: Choose a specific time each day to repeat your word-spells, ideally in the morning to set a positive tone for the day or at night to reinforce your intentions.
2. **Combine Word-Spells with Action**: Amplify the effect of each word-spell by pairing it with symbolic action, such as lighting a candle, holding a crystal, or focusing on a wealth symbol like a coin or talisman.
3. **Use Word-Spells as Reminders**: Write down your chosen wealth phrase or word-spell and place it where you'll see it throughout the day. Each time you see it, repeat the phrase in your mind or aloud, reinforcing the intention.

4. **Create a Personal Wealth Mantra**: If a particular word-spell resonates with you, use it as a mantra throughout your day. Repeat it during moments of quiet or before making financial decisions to align your energy with abundance.

DAILY WEALTH WORD-SPELL ROUTINE

This routine combines intention-setting, vibration, and visualisation with a selected word-spell. Dedicate 5–10 minutes each day to practice this exercise for maximum effect.

1. **Choose Your Word-Spell**: Select a word or phrase that resonates with your current financial goal, such as "Abracadabra" for manifestation, "Lux Fortunae" for luck, or "Creare Abundantiam" for abundance creation.
2. **Prepare Your Space**: Light a green or gold candle, hold a crystal or coin in your hand, and take a few deep breaths to center yourself.
3. **Repeat the Word-Spell with Intention**: Close your eyes and begin chanting the word-spell, feeling its vibration in your body. Imagine that each repetition amplifies the energy of your intention, creating a field of wealth around you.
4. **Visualise Your Goal**: As you chant, visualise your financial goal as if it has already been achieved. Feel the satisfaction and security that come with this wealth.
5. **Close with a Wealth Affirmation**: Finish by saying, "This wealth is mine; it flows to me easily and freely." Let the words resonate within you, reinforcing your alignment with abundance.

Ancient words of wealth act as vibrational tools, helping you align with the energy of abundance. By incorporating these words into daily routines, you can use sound and resonance to bridge the gap between intention and manifestation.

CHAPTER 3: DAILY WEALTH ALIGNMENT ROUTINE

THE POWER OF DAILY RITUAL IN WEALTH ALCHEMY

In wealth alchemy, the consistency of daily practices is key to maintaining alignment with prosperity. While larger rituals and spells set powerful intentions, it's the daily routine that reinforces these intentions, building a steady current of wealth-attracting energy. This chapter provides a structured daily routine for wealth alignment, incorporating visualisation, word-spells, and affirmations, along with grounding techniques to prepare you for the day's financial opportunities.

SETTING UP YOUR DAILY WEALTH ROUTINE

Consistency is crucial in wealth alchemy. By dedicating 5–15 minutes each morning and evening to this routine, you're effectively conditioning your mind, energy, and environment for abundance. This routine focuses on mental clarity, vibrational alignment, and creating a powerful intention that carries through your day.

Suggested Time Commitment: 5–15 minutes, once in the morning and once before bed.

MORNING WEALTH ALIGNMENT ROUTINE

1. Starting the Day with Intention (2 Minutes)

Begin your day by setting a clear intention to attract wealth. This intention acts as a "seed" of energy that will grow as you go about your day, anchoring you in a state of openness to financial opportunities.

How to Do It:

- Before getting out of bed, place your hand on your heart, close your eyes, and silently say, "I am open to wealth and prosperity today." Feel this intention filling your mind and body, radiating outward as a welcoming energy for abundance.
- Repeat the phrase three times, letting its energy resonate throughout your body.

2. Wealth Visualisation and Affirmation (3–5 Minutes)

Visualisation is a powerful method of imprinting your intentions into your subconscious mind. In this step, you'll visualise your ideal financial situation as though it already exists, focusing on both the image and the emotions associated with it.

How to Do It:

- Sit comfortably, close your eyes, and visualise your bank account or a specific financial goal. Imagine seeing the balance you desire or picture yourself achieving a financial milestone, like purchasing a house or making a profitable investment.
- Feel the emotions you'd experience—joy, security, confidence. Let these emotions fill your entire body, as though the wealth you envision is already yours.
- Close the visualisation by affirming, "I am a magnet for prosperity. Wealth flows to me effortlessly." Repeat this affirmation three times, anchoring your visualisation in your mind.

3. Word-Spell Chant (2 Minutes)

Select a word-spell from Chapter 2, such as *Abracadabra*, *Lux Fortunae*, or *Venite Divitiae*, to use as a daily mantra for wealth. This chant amplifies your intention and aligns your frequency with prosperity.

How to Do It:

- Choose one word-spell to use consistently for a week, allowing its energy to build. Sit comfortably, close your eyes, and begin chanting the word-spell softly, focusing on its vibration.
- Say the word-spell 9 times, feeling it resonate in your chest and spread through your body. Allow yourself to feel the energy of abundance growing with each repetition.

4. Physical Anchor: Wealth Symbol or Charm (1 Minute)

Using a physical symbol throughout the day keeps your mind aligned with your intention. This can be a small crystal, a coin, or a written phrase, something that reminds you of your wealth goals whenever you see or touch it.

How to Do It:

- Choose a small object that symbolises wealth for you, such as a citrine crystal, a coin, or a small piece of paper with your goal written on it.
- Hold the object in your hand after your visualisation and word-spell chant, affirming, "This symbolises my attraction to wealth and abundance." Keep it in your pocket, wallet, or workspace.

EVENING WEALTH REFLECTION AND RELEASE ROUTINE

At the end of the day, it's important to release any financial worries, reaffirm your wealth alignment, and express gratitude. This evening routine clears energetic blocks that may have accumulated, helping you enter a state of openness for the next day.

1. Financial Reflection and Gratitude (2–3 Minutes)

Reflect on the day's financial wins, no matter how small. This practice builds a sense of gratitude and keeps your mind focused on abundance rather than lack.

How to Do It:

- Sit comfortably, close your eyes, and mentally review any moments of financial positivity, whether it was receiving unexpected income, spending wisely, or learning a valuable financial lesson.
- Silently express gratitude for these experiences, affirming, "I am grateful for the wealth that flowed to me today." Repeat this affirmation three times to solidify a sense of thankfulness.

2. Release of Financial Worries (2–3 Minutes)

Letting go of worries at the end of the day ensures that you aren't carrying negative energy into the next day. This "clearing" process creates space for wealth energy to circulate.

How to Do It:

- Close your eyes, take a deep breath, and exhale slowly. With each exhale, imagine any financial stress, worry, or doubt leaving your body.

- As you breathe out, silently say, "I release all concerns around wealth. I am open to abundance." Repeat this for three deep breaths, feeling lighter with each exhale.

3. Wealth-Boosting Nightly Affirmation (1–2 Minutes)

End the day with a simple affirmation to reinforce your alignment with wealth as you prepare for rest. This affirmation helps to imprint positive financial beliefs in your subconscious, setting a strong foundation for the next day.

How to Do It:

- Sit or lie down comfortably, close your eyes, and repeat the following affirmation: "Wealth surrounds me, and my life is filled with prosperity." Repeat this affirmation 5 times, feeling each word resonate deeply.
- Visualise yourself surrounded by an energy field of abundance, and fall asleep with the feeling of prosperity.

CREATING A CONSISTENT ROUTINE

Consistency is the key to making these practices effective. Try to set aside the same time each day for your morning and evening routines, even if it's just five minutes. This routine can be adapted based on your schedule, but keeping some form of daily alignment practice helps reinforce your intentions and builds a resilient mindset focused on abundance.

CUSTOMISING YOUR ROUTINE

You can adjust this daily routine based on your evolving goals and the results you begin to notice. Here are a few ways to personalise it:

- **Weekly Word-Spell Focus**: Change your word-spell focus each week to keep the energy fresh. For example, use *Abracadabra* for one week and switch to *Lux Fortunae* the next.
- **Seasonal Wealth Symbol**: As the seasons change, update your wealth symbol or charm. Use objects that resonate with the season's energy, like a green leaf in spring or a small golden object in fall.
- **Journaling**: Keep a small wealth journal where you jot down reflections from your morning and evening routine. Over time, you'll see patterns emerge, giving you deeper insights into your alignment with wealth.

EXAMPLE DAILY WEALTH ROUTINE SUMMARY

Here's a quick summary of the daily routine to keep on hand:

Morning Routine

1. **Set Wealth Intention**: "I am open to wealth and prosperity today."
2. **Visualisation and Affirmation**: Visualise financial success and affirm, "I am a magnet for prosperity."
3. **Word-Spell Chant**: Choose a word-spell (e.g., *Lux Fortunae*) and chant it 9 times.
4. **Physical Anchor**: Carry a wealth symbol or charm with you throughout the day.

Evening Routine

1. **Reflection and Gratitude**: Recall moments of financial positivity and express gratitude.

2. **Release of Financial Worries**: Let go of financial stress through breathing and visualisation.
3. **Nightly Affirmation**: Affirm, "Wealth surrounds me, and my life is filled with prosperity."

Daily routines are the foundation of wealth alchemy. By integrating these simple practices each morning and evening, you continuously reinforce your alignment with prosperity. This chapter lays the groundwork for more advanced weekly and monthly rituals, which we'll explore in the following chapters. As you build consistency, you'll notice a shift in your mindset, energy, and financial opportunities, creating a steady flow of wealth that aligns with your life's goals.

CHAPTER 4: WEEKLY WEALTH RITUALS AND PRACTICES

THE POWER OF WEEKLY WEALTH RITUALS

While daily routines build consistent wealth energy, weekly rituals allow for more focused, intentional work. Setting aside time each week for wealth practices helps you dive deeper into your goals, refresh your intentions, and clear any energetic blocks that may have built up. These practices are designed to create a surge of energy, amplifying your wealth alignment and attracting new opportunities.

Suggested Time Commitment: 20–30 minutes once a week, ideally on the same day each week to build a rhythm.

1. Golden Path Candle Ritual

The Golden Path Candle Ritual uses candles, symbols, and affirmations to create a pathway for wealth energy to flow into your life. This ritual combines the principles of intention-setting, visualisation, and vibrational alignment, helping you channel focused wealth energy for the week ahead.

Tools Needed:

- A green or gold candle (green represents growth, and gold represents wealth)
- Basil leaves (symbolic of prosperity)
- A small handful of coins or a single gold-colored coin (symbolising financial success)
- A piece of paper and pen

Steps for the Golden Path Candle Ritual:

1. **Prepare Your Space**: Find a quiet place where you won't be disturbed. Set up a small table or surface with the candle, basil leaves, coins, and paper.
2. **Set Your Wealth Intention**: On the piece of paper, write down your wealth goal for the week. Be specific and clear, such as "I attract new financial opportunities that increase my income by [amount]." Fold the paper and place it under the candle.
3. **Create the Wealth Pathway**: Place the basil leaves and coins in a line leading to the candle, symbolising a path toward your financial goal. Visualise this pathway as an open road, free of obstacles, leading directly to prosperity.
4. **Light the Candle and Chant**: Light the candle and chant, "This flame guides the path to my wealth. Prosperity flows easily and abundantly." Repeat this chant three times, allowing each repetition to build your focus.
5. **Visualise Your Goal**: With the candle burning, close your eyes and visualise yourself achieving the financial goal you wrote down. Imagine yourself walking along the "wealth pathway," arriving at a place of success and financial security. See yourself filled with confidence and peace as you reach your goal.
6. **Seal the Ritual**: When you feel ready, extinguish the candle and say, "The path to wealth is open, and prosperity flows to me." Leave the setup in place for the rest of the week as a reminder of your intention, or, if space is limited, store the items in a small box or pouch.

2. Sacred Geometry and Wealth Grids

Using sacred geometry symbols like the Flower of Life or Metatron's Cube, a wealth grid creates a structured space that amplifies your financial intentions. This practice is ideal for setting up a long-term wealth "magnet" in your workspace or home, maintaining consistent alignment with abundance.

Tools Needed:

- A printed or drawn image of a sacred geometry symbol (Flower of Life or Metatron's Cube are ideal)
- Crystals associated with wealth (e.g., citrine, pyrite, green aventurine)
- A small green or gold object (optional) for added symbolism

Steps for Creating a Wealth Grid:

1. **Choose a Space**: Find a flat surface in a part of your home or workspace dedicated to your financial goals. Clean the area, clearing it of any clutter to maintain focused energy.
2. **Place the Sacred Geometry Symbol**: Lay the sacred geometry symbol on the surface. This acts as the foundation of your wealth grid, structuring energy in a way that invites abundance.
3. **Arrange Crystals and Objects**: Place the crystals and any other wealth symbols (such as a coin or small gold item) around the geometry symbol in a pattern that feels balanced. Citrine, pyrite, and aventurine are powerful choices for attracting wealth and amplifying prosperity energy.
4. **Set Your Wealth Intention**: Stand or sit in front of the grid, close your eyes, and state your financial goal aloud, clearly and with conviction. Visualise wealth energy radiating from the crystals, moving through the geometry pattern, and spreading outward to attract abundance.
5. **Activate the Grid**: Lightly touch each item on the grid, saying, "I activate this wealth grid to attract prosperity,

success, and abundance." Allow your hands to rest briefly on the symbol, feeling the energy of wealth build and expand.

6. **Maintain the Grid**: Refresh your intention each week by spending a few moments with the grid, visualising your wealth goal, and reactivating the energy. This consistency helps sustain the energy and alignment of the grid.

3. Weekly Energy Clearing Ritual

Energy clearing removes any blockages, resistance, or negativity surrounding wealth that may have built up over the week. This ritual creates an open, clear channel for prosperity, allowing abundance to flow freely without obstruction.

Tools Needed:

- Incense or sage for smudging (sandalwood or sage are ideal for clearing)
- A bowl of salt (for grounding and clearing energy)
- Optional: small bell or chime for sound clearing

Steps for the Energy Clearing Ritual:

1. **Prepare Your Space**: Set up in a quiet room. Light the incense or sage, and allow the smoke to move around the space, clearing away any stagnant energy.
2. **Ground Yourself**: Stand or sit comfortably, close your eyes, and take a few deep breaths. Visualise yourself as deeply connected to the earth, with roots extending down from your feet.
3. **Smudging and Clearing**: Use the incense or sage to gently smudge your body, moving from head to feet, focusing on areas where you feel tension or resistance. As you move, say, "I release all blocks and open myself to the flow of wealth."

4. **Sound Clearing (Optional)**: If you have a small bell or chime, ring it around your space to break up any lingering stagnant energy, especially in corners and near doorways. Visualise the sound carrying away any heaviness or resistance to abundance.
5. **Salt Grounding**: Place a pinch of salt in each corner of the room as a way of grounding the space. Salt is believed to absorb negativity, leaving the environment clear and open to positive energy.
6. **Closing Intention**: Once you've cleared the space, sit quietly for a few moments and affirm, "I am open to receiving wealth. My energy is clear, my path is open, and prosperity flows to me."

4. Reflection and Goal-Setting for the Week Ahead

Weekly reflection and goal-setting allow you to check in with your financial goals, review your progress, and set fresh intentions. This practice reinforces your alignment with abundance, giving you a clear focus for the week ahead.

Steps for Weekly Reflection and Goal-Setting:

1. **Review Financial Progress**: Set aside 5–10 minutes to review the past week's financial experiences. Reflect on any progress, lessons, or insights related to wealth. Write these reflections in a wealth journal, noting areas where you felt aligned with prosperity or experienced financial growth.
2. **Set a Financial Goal**: Based on your reflection, set a specific goal for the upcoming week. This goal could be as simple as saving a certain amount, finding new investment opportunities, or making progress on a larger financial target.

3. **Affirm Your Goal**: Write your goal at the top of a fresh page in your wealth journal. Close your eyes and affirm, "I am focused, clear, and open to new opportunities. I set this goal with confidence and trust in my ability to achieve it."
4. **Visualisation**: Visualise yourself successfully meeting your goal. Picture the positive emotions, sense of accomplishment, and benefits that come with achieving this milestone.

EXAMPLE WEEKLY WEALTH ROUTINE SUMMARY

Here's a quick summary of the weekly routine to keep on hand:

1. **Golden Path Candle Ritual**: Set a specific wealth intention for the week, light a candle, and visualise your path to prosperity.
2. **Wealth Grid Activation**: Arrange a sacred geometry wealth grid with crystals and symbols, activate it, and revisit it weekly to maintain focus.
3. **Energy Clearing Ritual**: Clear any negative energy around you and release financial resistance using smudging, salt, and sound.
4. **Weekly Reflection and Goal-Setting**: Reflect on financial growth, set a new goal, and visualise your success.

Weekly wealth rituals create a powerful alignment with prosperity, helping you deepen your financial focus and clear any blocks that may arise. By integrating these practices into your routine, you build a steady, resilient foundation for attracting wealth. In the next chapter, we'll expand on these practices by introducing specific word-spells and incantations, allowing you to tap further into the ancient power of language to enhance your wealth alignment.

CHAPTER 5: WORD-SPELLS AND ANCIENT INCANTATIONS

HARNESSING THE POWER OF WORDS FOR WEALTH

In ancient traditions, words were seen as tools of creation, with specific sounds, phrases, and incantations capable of shaping reality. This idea is embedded in magical practices across cultures, where words are used to focus intent and summon energies aligned with desired outcomes. Each word-spell in this chapter has a rich history of association with wealth, prosperity, and abundance, and is designed to resonate with the energy of prosperity when spoken with intention.

The power of word-spells lies in their vibrational frequency. When you speak these words with conviction, they activate subtle energies within and around you, aligning your personal vibration with the energy of abundance. This chapter provides detailed instructions for using these word-spells as part of your daily and weekly practices.

KEY WORD-SPELLS FOR WEALTH

Below are specific word-spells selected for their traditional association with wealth. Each entry includes the word's origin, meaning, and step-by-step guidance on how to incorporate it into your routine.

1. Abracadabra

Meaning: "I create as I speak." The word Abracadabra has roots in ancient Aramaic and is one of the most widely recognised magical words. It was traditionally used in rituals as a protective word but also carries the power of manifestation. In the context of wealth alchemy, Abracadabra is used as a creative phrase to turn your thoughts into reality.

How to Use Abracadabra for Wealth:

- **Daily Wealth Chant**: Choose a specific financial goal (e.g., "I attract $5,000"). Write this goal down on a piece of paper and place it in front of you. Close your eyes and visualise your goal as if it has already manifested.
- **Chanting Practice**: Begin chanting "Abracadabra" slowly and deliberately, letting each syllable resonate throughout your body. Imagine the sound activating your intention and creating a pathway for wealth to flow to you.
- **Repetition**: Repeat "Abracadabra" nine times, each time with more conviction. Conclude by affirming, "As I speak it, so it becomes." Feel the energy of your words aligning with your financial goal.

2. Lux Fortunae (Light of Fortune)

Meaning: Latin for "Light of Fortune," Lux Fortunae is used to attract luck, fortune, and financial blessings. This word-spell aligns you with the energy of good fortune, helping you radiate an inviting aura that draws wealth and success.

How to Use Lux Fortunae for Wealth:

- **Candle Ritual**: Light a green or gold candle. Close your eyes, place your hands over your heart, and chant, "Lux Fortunae, Lux Fortunae, Lux Fortunae—light of fortune, shine upon me."
- **Visualisation**: Imagine a golden light expanding from your chest, filling your body with the energy of luck and financial

blessings. Visualise this light radiating outward, attracting wealth opportunities toward you.
- **Repetition**: Chant "Lux Fortunae" nine times, each time feeling more connected to the energy of fortune. End with the affirmation, "I am a beacon of fortune and wealth."

3. Venite Divitiae (Come, Riches)

Meaning: Another phrase rooted in Latin, "Venite Divitiae" translates directly to "Come, riches." This incantation is a powerful call to abundance, inviting wealth into your life.

How to Use Venite Divitiae for Wealth:

- **Simple Daily Invocation**: Write "Venite Divitiae" on a small piece of paper. Place it under a green candle, light the candle, and visualise financial abundance flowing into your life.
- **Chanting Practice**: Repeat "Venite Divitiae" twelve times, each time feeling wealth and abundance coming closer. Visualise money, success, and resources gathering around you as you chant.
- **Affirmation**: After chanting, say, "By these words, wealth is drawn to me. My life is filled with riches and success." Let the candle burn down completely if possible, and keep the paper as a charm to carry with you.

4. Solvo et Colligo (I Release and I Gather)

Meaning: Translating to "I release and I gather," this Latin phrase represents the concept of letting go of scarcity-based thoughts and attracting abundance. It aligns with the alchemical principle of release and accumulation, which helps remove blocks to prosperity and draws wealth into your life.

How to Use Solvo et Colligo for Wealth:

- **Breathwork with Chanting**: Find a quiet place to sit comfortably. Begin by closing your eyes and taking slow, deep breaths. As you exhale, say "Solvo," and imagine releasing all fears, doubts, or scarcity-based beliefs.
- **Gathering Wealth**: On each inhale, say "Colligo," visualising wealth, abundance, and opportunities gathering around you. See yourself surrounded by prosperity.
- **Rhythmic Repetition**: Repeat "Solvo et Colligo" in a rhythm, alternating between release and gathering for about five minutes. Finish by saying, "With these words, I release all lack and gather endless wealth."

5. Creare Abundantiam (Create Abundance)

Meaning: Latin for "Create abundance," Creare Abundantiam is a direct invocation for generating and attracting prosperity into your life. This phrase is used to cultivate an active state of wealth creation, focusing both on attracting and sustaining abundance.

How to Use Creare Abundantiam for Wealth:

- **Visualisation with Objects**: Light a green or gold candle and place a small bowl of coins or crystals (such as citrine or pyrite) in front of you. Visualise these items as symbols of wealth, multiplying and increasing as you focus on them.
- **Chanting Practice**: Chant "Creare Abundantiam" nine times, visualising more wealth flowing toward you and the coins or crystals multiplying. Feel the energy of abundance surrounding you.
- **Affirmation**: Conclude with the affirmation, "My abundance is created and flows freely." Keep the bowl of

coins or crystals in a place of prominence to symbolise your growing wealth.

USING WORD-SPELLS IN DAILY LIFE

The following tips will help you incorporate these word-spells into your daily and weekly routines for maximum effect:

1. **Daily Word-Spell Ritual**: Choose one word-spell to focus on for the day. Each morning, spend a few minutes chanting it and visualising your wealth goals. Repeat it throughout the day whenever you need a boost of alignment with prosperity.
2. **Weekly Word-Spell Focus**: Select a specific word-spell for each week, allowing its energy to build over time. Use it in your weekly wealth rituals, such as during the Golden Path Candle Ritual or Sacred Geometry Wealth Grid, to deepen your connection to the word's energy.
3. **Journaling with Word-Spells**: At the end of each day, write down any insights or experiences related to the word-spell you used. Reflect on how it affected your mindset, actions, or any financial opportunities you encountered.
4. **Word-Spells as Mantras**: If a specific word resonates strongly with you, consider using it as a mantra for meditation or while doing routine tasks. This practice reinforces your alignment with wealth and can be a grounding reminder of your financial intentions.

CREATING A PERSONAL WEALTH WORD-SPELL

While ancient words carry established energies, you may find that creating your own wealth word-spell adds a personal layer of meaning and alignment. Here's a step-by-step exercise for creating your own word-spell:

1. **Identify Your Financial Goal**: Start by defining a specific financial intention. For example, "I want to increase my income by 25%" or "I want to attract new investment opportunities."
2. **Choose Words or Phrases that Resonate**: Combine words that resonate with your goal and create a short, memorable phrase. For example, you might combine words like "flow," "wealth," and "strength" to create a phrase such as "Wealth flows to me with strength."
3. **Infuse the Phrase with Intention**: Close your eyes and repeat your new word-spell, letting it resonate deeply. Imagine it carrying the energy of your goal, aligning your vibration with the frequency of prosperity.
4. **Use it in Your Routine**: Incorporate your personalised word-spell into your daily and weekly rituals. Chant it during meditation, write it in your journal, or pair it with a wealth ritual to anchor it more fully.

EXAMPLE WORD-SPELL ROUTINE

Here's a sample routine incorporating word-spells into a structured practice:

1. **Morning Chant**: Begin each morning by chanting your chosen word-spell nine times, focusing on its energy and meaning. Visualise your financial goals as you chant.
2. **Daily Mantra**: Throughout the day, repeat your word-spell whenever you need to refocus or reinforce your alignment with wealth.
3. **Evening Reflection**: At the end of the day, reflect on how your word-spell influenced your thoughts, actions, or any financial insights. Write any reflections in your wealth journal to track your progress.

Word-spells are powerful tools for focusing intention, creating alignment, and drawing prosperity into your life. Each word or phrase resonates at a frequency associated with wealth, and using them consistently in your daily and weekly practices builds a strong energetic foundation for abundance.

CHAPTER 6: MONTHLY AND SEASONAL WEALTH RITUALS

ALIGNING WITH NATURAL CYCLES FOR WEALTH

In ancient practices, natural cycles—like the phases of the moon and the changing seasons—were considered powerful allies in manifestation. By working with these cycles, we can amplify our intentions, create a sense of renewal, and establish a rhythm that keeps us attuned to prosperity. Monthly and seasonal wealth rituals encourage us to connect with the broader energies of nature, helping to anchor and refresh our financial intentions.

This chapter includes monthly rituals aligned with the moon phases and seasonal practices that align with the unique energies of each season. These rituals are designed to be practiced at specific times, giving you a sense of progression and renewal in your wealth journey.

MONTHLY WEALTH RITUALS WITH THE MOON CYCLE

The moon has four main phases: New Moon, Waxing Moon, Full Moon, and Waning Moon. Each phase has distinct energy that can be used to support your wealth goals. Working with the moon cycle creates a rhythm that reinforces your financial intentions, helping you progress steadily and consistently toward abundance.

New Moon: Setting Wealth Intentions

The New Moon is a time of fresh starts and setting intentions. This phase is ideal for clarifying new financial goals and planting the "seeds" of wealth you wish to manifest over the coming weeks.

How to Do It:

1. **Preparation**: Begin by creating a quiet, sacred space. Light a green or gold candle to represent prosperity.
2. **Write Down Your Intentions**: On a piece of paper, write down your wealth goals for the upcoming month. Be specific—whether it's attracting new clients, increasing savings, or hitting an investment target.
3. **Visualise**: Close your eyes and visualise these goals as if they've already been achieved. Feel the satisfaction and joy associated with each intention.
4. **Chant a Wealth Word-Spell**: Use a word-spell like "Abracadabra" or "Venite Divitiae" to affirm your intention. Repeat it 9 times, focusing on the energy of creation and new beginnings.
5. **Seal the Intention**: Conclude by saying, "With this new moon, I plant the seeds of my prosperity. Wealth flows to me, and my goals manifest with ease."

Waxing Moon: Building Wealth Energy

As the moon grows from New to Full (waxing phase), its energy supports growth and expansion. This is the ideal time to take action on your financial goals and strengthen your focus on prosperity.

How to Do It:

1. **Revisit Your Intentions**: Reflect on the intentions you set during the New Moon. Write down any progress you've made and reaffirm your commitment.
2. **Create a Wealth Grid**: Set up a simple wealth grid using crystals (such as citrine or pyrite) arranged in a pattern

around your written intention. Visualise the grid amplifying your wealth energy.
3. **Daily Affirmation**: Each day during the waxing moon, affirm, "My wealth grows each day. I am aligned with prosperity."
4. **Celebrate Small Wins**: Acknowledge any small successes or positive changes related to your wealth goals. Each time you recognise progress, you reinforce your alignment with abundance.

Full Moon: Celebrating Abundance and Manifestation

The Full Moon is the peak of the moon's energy, representing completion, manifestation, and abundance. This is the time to celebrate financial gains, express gratitude, and amplify your wealth energy.

How to Do It:

1. **Gather Wealth Symbols**: Collect items that symbolise abundance for you, such as coins, crystals, or a gold object.
2. **Gratitude Ritual**: Sit quietly with these items and express gratitude for any wealth that has come into your life, no matter how small. Focus on feelings of appreciation and contentment.
3. **Chanting and Visualisation**: Chant "Lux Fortunae" or "Creare Abundantiam" nine times, visualising wealth surrounding you. Imagine the Full Moon amplifying your intentions and creating a strong magnetic field for abundance.
4. **Celebrate with a Gesture**: Do something symbolic to celebrate your wealth journey. This could be a small treat or

gift for yourself, symbolising the rewards of your financial growth.

Waning Moon: Releasing Financial Blocks

As the moon moves from Full to New (waning phase), it's an ideal time to release any obstacles, limiting beliefs, or financial stress. This phase is about clearing and making space for new opportunities.

How to Do It:

1. **Reflect and Identify Blocks**: Reflect on any challenges or limiting beliefs that surfaced during the month. Write them down on a piece of paper.
2. **Release with Breathwork**: Hold the paper and take a few deep breaths. As you exhale, imagine each limiting belief dissolving. Say, "I release all that hinders my wealth."
3. **Burn or Tear the Paper**: Safely burn or tear the paper, symbolising the release of these blocks. Visualise yourself feeling lighter, with a clear path to financial success.
4. **Affirm New Possibilities**: End with the affirmation, "I am open to new opportunities, and wealth flows to me easily and freely."

SEASONAL WEALTH RITUALS

Aligning with the seasons allows you to adapt your wealth practices to the natural flow of energy throughout the year. Each season brings unique qualities that can enhance your alignment with abundance.

Spring Equinox: Planting Seeds of Prosperity

Spring is a time of renewal, growth, and new beginnings. Use this energy to set long-term financial goals and plant the "seeds" of prosperity.

How to Do It:

1. **Set Long-Term Financial Goals**: Reflect on your wealth goals for the coming year. Write down these goals as "seeds" you intend to nurture.
2. **Plant a Symbolic Seed**: Take a small potted plant or seedling and plant it in fresh soil. As you plant it, say, "I plant the seeds of my prosperity and nurture my wealth."
3. **Daily Care**: Care for the plant over the season, symbolising your commitment to nurturing your financial goals. Each time you water it, visualise your wealth growing.

Summer Solstice: Celebrating Growth and Expansion

The Summer Solstice is the longest day of the year, representing peak growth and expansion. This is a powerful time to amplify your wealth energy and celebrate your financial progress.

How to Do It:

1. **Create a Wealth Altar:** Set up an altar with symbols of abundance, such as gold coins, citrine crystals, and fresh flowers. This altar serves as a focal point for your wealth energy.

2. **Affirm Growth**: Stand before your altar and affirm, "My wealth grows steadily and abundantly. I celebrate the prosperity in my life."
3. **Journaling Reflection**: Write down any significant financial milestones you've reached so far this year. Celebrate these wins, recognising how far you've come.

Autumn Equinox: Harvesting Rewards

The Autumn Equinox is a time of harvest, symbolising the rewards of your efforts. Use this energy to assess your financial growth and harvest the benefits of your wealth journey.

How to Do It:

1. **Reflect on Achievements**: Take time to review your financial progress for the year. Write down any rewards you've "harvested" and express gratitude for them.
2. **Symbolic Offering**: Place a small offering on your wealth altar, such as fruit or a symbolic gift, as a token of appreciation for the abundance in your life.
3. **Grounding Exercise**: Connect with the earth by standing barefoot outdoors if possible. Visualise your wealth as deeply rooted, growing stronger and more stable each day.

Winter Solstice: Reflecting and Setting Intentions for the New Year

Winter is a time of rest, reflection, and introspection. The Winter Solstice, the longest night of the year, is ideal for reviewing your financial journey, releasing what no longer serves you, and setting intentions for the coming year.

How to Do It:

1. **Year-End Reflection**: Reflect on your financial journey over the past year. Write down what worked, what didn't, and what you've learned.
2. **Release and Renew**: Write down any limiting beliefs or financial habits you wish to leave behind. Safely burn or bury this paper as a symbolic release.
3. **Set New Intentions**: Light a candle and set new financial intentions for the coming year, saying, "I welcome the light of prosperity into my life. My wealth journey is blessed."

EXAMPLE MONTHLY AND SEASONAL WEALTH RITUAL SUMMARY

Here's a quick summary of the monthly and seasonal wealth practices:

Monthly Moon Cycle

- **New Moon**: Set financial intentions.
- **Waxing Moon**: Build energy and take action.
- **Full Moon**: Celebrate and amplify wealth.
- **Waning Moon**: Release blocks and limitations.

Seasonal Practices

- **Spring Equinox**: Plant seeds of long-term prosperity.
- **Summer Solstice**: Celebrate growth and expansion.

- **Autumn Equinox**: Harvest the rewards of your financial journey.
- **Winter Solstice**: Reflect, release, and set new intentions for the year.

Monthly and seasonal wealth rituals create a powerful synergy with natural cycles, helping you align with prosperity on a deeper level. By working with the energies of the moon phases and seasonal shifts, you create a steady rhythm that supports your financial intentions and enhances your wealth journey. In the next chapter, we'll explore alchemical practices for inner transformation, allowing you to cultivate a mindset and energy that naturally attract abundance.

CHAPTER 7: ALCHEMICAL PRACTICES FOR INNER WEALTH

THE INNER TRANSFORMATION OF WEALTH

Alchemy has long been associated with the transformation of base metals into gold, but this ancient science is also a metaphor for inner transformation. In the same way alchemists refined raw materials into pure elements, we can transform limiting beliefs, self-doubt, and scarcity mindsets into qualities that naturally attract wealth—such as confidence, trust, and a deep sense of abundance.

Inner wealth transformation is the process of refining your thoughts, emotions, and beliefs to resonate at the frequency of prosperity. These practices serve as a foundation for all other wealth rituals, as they help clear internal barriers and create a mindset that supports lasting financial growth.

THE ALCHEMICAL STAGES OF INNER TRANSFORMATION

Traditional alchemy describes several stages of transformation. Each stage represents a step in the process of turning raw material into gold, and we can apply these stages to our personal development journey. Here, we'll explore how each stage corresponds to qualities necessary for attracting wealth.

1. Nigredo (Blackening) – Releasing Limiting Beliefs

The first stage, Nigredo, represents purification and the breakdown of old forms. In personal alchemy, this is the process of recognising and releasing limiting beliefs about wealth. These beliefs are often subconscious and may stem from past experiences or cultural conditioning.

How to Practice Nigredo for Wealth:

- **Identify Limiting Beliefs**: Spend time reflecting on beliefs you hold about money. Write down any thoughts that surface, especially those that feel restrictive or negative (e.g., "Money is hard to come by" or "I am not worthy of wealth").
- **Reframe Negative Beliefs**: For each limiting belief, create an empowering counter-statement. For example, replace "Money is hard to come by" with "I am open to financial abundance."
- **Release Ritual**: Safely burn or tear up the paper containing your limiting beliefs, visualising them dissolving. As you release them, say, "I let go of beliefs that do not serve my highest wealth."

2. Albedo (Whitening) – Cultivating Clarity and Purity

The Albedo stage represents clarity, cleansing, and illumination. Here, we work on clearing away emotional attachments to financial fears and gaining clarity on our wealth goals. This stage is about refining your vision of abundance and ensuring it aligns with your values.

How to Practice Albedo for Wealth:

- **Define Your True Wealth Goals**: Write down what financial success means to you, beyond just accumulating money. Consider how wealth will improve your life and allow you to contribute positively to the world.
- **Visualisation Exercise**: Sit in a quiet space, close your eyes, and visualise your ideal financial state. Imagine this state bringing you a sense of clarity, peace, and purpose.

- **Affirm Clarity**: Affirm, "I am clear about my wealth goals. My path to prosperity is pure and aligned with my purpose." Repeat this daily as a reminder to keep your vision focused.

3. Citrinitas (Yellowing) – Awakening Confidence and Action

Citrinitas is the stage of awakening, energy, and active engagement. In this phase, we embrace confidence and take aligned action to pursue our financial goals. This stage encourages us to embody the qualities of courage, decisiveness, and empowerment in our wealth journey.

How to Practice Citrinitas for Wealth:

- **Action List**: Create a list of specific actions you can take to further your financial goals, such as saving, investing, or exploring new income opportunities.
- **Empowerment Visualisation**: Close your eyes and visualise yourself confidently making financial decisions. Picture each action you take bringing you closer to your goals, with ease and assurance.
- **Affirm Confidence**: Stand in front of a mirror, look into your eyes, and affirm, "I am confident and capable. I take decisive actions that lead to wealth and prosperity."

4. Rubedo (Reddening) – Integrating and Embodying Prosperity

The final stage, Rubedo, represents the integration of all previous stages and the realisation of goals. In wealth alchemy, Rubedo is about fully embodying prosperity as a natural state. By this stage, you've transformed limiting beliefs, gained clarity, and taken confident actions. Now, you live as if wealth is an inherent part of your life.

How to Practice Rubedo for Wealth:

- **Gratitude Practice**: Each day, express gratitude for the wealth you already have, no matter how small. Gratitude creates a powerful state of contentment and opens you to receive more.
- **Living as Abundant**: Act "as if" you are already financially abundant. Treat yourself to small rewards, maintain a mindset of generosity, and make decisions from a place of security and prosperity.
- **Affirm Embodiment**: Affirm, "I live in a state of abundance. Wealth flows to me naturally, and I embody prosperity in all I do." Repeat this daily to reinforce your alignment with wealth.

PRACTICAL EXERCISES FOR INNER TRANSFORMATION

The following exercises help you work through each alchemical stage on a practical level. You can incorporate these into your daily or weekly routines as needed.

Journaling Through the Alchemical Stages

Journaling is a powerful tool for self-reflection and growth. Use it to document your progress through each stage, exploring your beliefs, goals, and actions as you move toward greater alignment with prosperity.

1. **Nigredo**: Write down any limiting beliefs you uncover about money. Note how these beliefs have impacted your financial experiences.

2. **Albedo**: Define your vision of wealth. Describe what financial success looks like and how it aligns with your values.
3. **Citrinitas**: List the actions you plan to take toward your financial goals. Document each step and how it brings you closer to abundance.
4. **Rubedo**: Write about how you feel embodying wealth. Describe small ways you act "as if" you are financially abundant and the effects you notice.

Inner Wealth Meditation

This guided meditation aligns your mind and energy with each stage of the alchemical transformation. Practicing this meditation regularly helps reinforce your inner wealth alignment.

1. **Find a Comfortable Position**: Sit or lie down in a quiet space, close your eyes, and take a few deep breaths.
2. **Nigredo**: Focus on any limiting beliefs you wish to release. Visualise these beliefs as dark clouds, gradually dissipating with each exhale.
3. **Albedo**: Picture a bright, white light filling you, representing clarity and purpose. See this light illuminating your financial goals.
4. **Citrinitas**: Visualise yourself taking confident, bold actions toward wealth. Feel a surge of energy as you imagine success in each endeavor.
5. **Rubedo**: Imagine yourself living in a state of complete abundance. Feel the contentment and fulfillment of embodying wealth. Repeat, "I am abundance."

Daily Alchemical Affirmations

Using affirmations aligned with each stage reinforces your transformation process. Repeat these daily, ideally during your morning routine, to set a strong tone for the day.

- **Nigredo**: "I release all beliefs that do not serve my highest wealth."
- **Albedo**: "I am clear about my wealth goals and aligned with my purpose."
- **Citrinitas**: "I take confident actions that lead to financial success."
- **Rubedo**: "I embody abundance. Wealth flows to me naturally."

BUILDING A RESILIENT WEALTH MINDSET

As you progress through each alchemical stage, you'll cultivate a mindset that is both resilient and open to wealth. This process helps you release scarcity mindsets, develop clarity and purpose, and strengthen your confidence in financial matters. Below are additional tips for building a strong, prosperous mindset:

1. **Embrace Growth over Perfection**: Inner transformation is a journey. Focus on continuous growth, rather than perfection, as you refine your mindset and energy for wealth.
2. **Practice Patience and Trust**: Trust that each stage of the process brings you closer to lasting prosperity. Even when results aren't immediate, believe in the gradual transformation unfolding.
3. **Celebrate Small Wins**: Acknowledge and celebrate small achievements along the way. Each success strengthens your belief in your ability to attract and sustain wealth.

EXAMPLE INNER WEALTH TRANSFORMATION ROUTINE

Here's a sample routine to incorporate inner transformation practices into your daily life:

1. **Morning Affirmation**: Choose an affirmation aligned with your current alchemical stage. Repeat it three times to start your day with intention.
2. **Reflection or Meditation**: Spend 5–10 minutes meditating on your current stage or journaling any insights that arise. Focus on releasing, gaining clarity, building confidence, or embodying wealth, depending on your needs.
3. **Evening Gratitude**: At the end of each day, write down three things you're grateful for, focusing on both tangible and intangible wealth. This practice reinforces a mindset of abundance.

The alchemical practices for inner transformation are powerful tools for creating a resilient, abundant mindset. By working through the stages of Nigredo, Albedo, Citrinitas, and Rubedo, you refine your beliefs, gain clarity, embrace confident action, and fully embody prosperity. This internal alignment provides a stable foundation for wealth attraction, making it easier to achieve and sustain financial growth. In the next chapter, we'll discuss how to create a personalised wealth path by combining the practices you've learned into a structured, sustainable routine that aligns with your unique goals.

CHAPTER 8: CREATING A PERSONALISED WEALTH PATH

DESIGNING YOUR WEALTH PATH

Each person's journey to financial prosperity is unique, shaped by individual goals, values, and circumstances. While the rituals, word-spells, and practices covered in this book provide the foundation, customising them to fit your personal needs ensures they resonate more deeply and effectively.

In this chapter, we'll explore how to design a wealth path that combines daily, weekly, monthly, and seasonal practices. By creating a routine that aligns with your intentions and lifestyle, you'll cultivate a consistent flow of wealth energy, allowing you to stay focused, track your progress, and make adjustments as needed.

1. DEFINING YOUR WEALTH GOALS

Start by clarifying your specific financial goals. A personalised wealth path begins with knowing exactly what you're aiming to achieve and why it matters to you. Your goals might range from increasing income to building savings, making investments, or achieving financial independence.

Steps for Defining Wealth Goals:

- **Create Clear, Measurable Goals**: Define your goals as specifically as possible. For example, instead of saying, "I want to make more money," specify, "I want to increase my income by 20% within the next six months."
- **Align with Your Values**: Consider why these goals are important to you. Aligning financial intentions with your

values creates a sense of purpose that supports long-term motivation.
- **Set Short, Medium, and Long-Term Goals**: Break down your financial aspirations into short-term (1–3 months), medium-term (6–12 months), and long-term (1–5 years) goals. This structure helps you maintain focus and track your progress over time.

Example Wealth Goals:

- **Short-Term**: Save an extra $500 each month.
- **Medium-Term**: Build a six-month emergency fund.
- **Long-Term**: Purchase a property or reach financial independence.

2. STRUCTURING YOUR WEALTH ROUTINE

To ensure you're consistently aligned with prosperity, design a routine that includes daily, weekly, monthly, and seasonal practices. Integrating various practices provides a balanced approach, allowing you to remain engaged without becoming overwhelmed.

Daily Practices

- **Morning Wealth Alignment**: Begin each day with a short intention-setting routine, incorporating affirmations, visualisations, or word-spells to align with wealth energy.
- **Midday Wealth Check-In**: Take a moment midday to reaffirm your financial goals, using a word-spell or mantra like "Venite Divitiae" to maintain focus.
- **Evening Gratitude and Reflection**: End each day by noting any progress toward your wealth goals and expressing gratitude. This practice builds a mindset focused on abundance and appreciation.

Weekly Practices

- **Golden Path Candle Ritual**: Perform a weekly ritual, such as the Golden Path Candle Ritual, to reaffirm your financial intentions for the week and clear any resistance.
- **Energy Clearing and Reflection**: Spend time clearing your energy and reflecting on the week's financial experiences. Note any obstacles, wins, or new insights.

Monthly Practices

- **New Moon Wealth Intention Setting**: Use the new moon to set fresh financial intentions for the month, focusing on one or two specific goals.
- **Full Moon Gratitude Ritual**: During the full moon, celebrate financial achievements and express gratitude for any progress. This ritual amplifies the energy of abundance.

Seasonal Practices

- **Spring Equinox Goal Setting**: In spring, set major wealth goals for the year and "plant" the intentions you'll nurture throughout the coming months.
- **Autumn Equinox Harvest Ritual**: In autumn, reflect on your achievements and assess what has worked well. Use this time to adjust any goals or approaches that need refining.

3. TRACKING PROGRESS AND REFLECTING ON YOUR WEALTH PATH

Tracking your journey helps you see tangible evidence of your progress, reinforcing your alignment with wealth. Use a wealth journal to document your goals, insights, and achievements.

Wealth Journal Setup

- **Intention Section**: Dedicate the beginning of your journal to writing down your financial goals and intentions. Include both specific goals and any overarching intentions or affirmations, such as "I am open to financial abundance."
- **Daily Reflections**: Each day, jot down any observations related to wealth, such as financial wins, new insights, or areas of improvement.
- **Weekly Review**: At the end of each week, review your entries. Summarise any key takeaways, successes, or challenges. Note any adjustments needed for the following week.
- **Monthly Reflection**: Use a larger section at the end of each month to assess progress toward your goals, celebrate achievements, and set intentions for the next month.

Reflective Questions to Guide Your Path

- **What progress have I made toward my wealth goals this week/month?**
- **What insights or lessons did I learn about wealth this week/month?**
- **Are there any limiting beliefs that surfaced and need releasing?**
- **What new opportunities am I open to for increasing my wealth?**

4. Maintaining Alignment and Staying Motivated

Creating and sustaining a wealth path requires consistent alignment and motivation. Here are techniques to help you stay engaged with your practice over the long term:

Celebrate Milestones and Small Wins

- Acknowledge even small financial achievements. Celebrating these moments reinforces a positive mindset and builds momentum. For example, reward yourself when you save a certain amount or hit an investment goal.

Revisit Goals Periodically

- Regularly check in with your financial goals and adjust as needed. Your wealth path may evolve as your life circumstances and values change, and it's essential to keep your goals relevant and inspiring.

Practice Patience and Faith

- Trust that the wealth practices you're engaging in will yield results, even if progress seems gradual. Consistent effort and faith in the process are key to long-term financial growth. Remind yourself, "I am on a steady path to prosperity."

5. DEVELOPING RESILIENCE ON YOUR WEALTH PATH

Challenges are a natural part of any journey, and building resilience is essential for maintaining steady progress. Use these techniques to help you navigate setbacks with ease and stay committed to your wealth path.

Embrace a Growth Mindset

- Approach challenges with curiosity and a growth mindset. Instead of seeing setbacks as failures, view them as opportunities to learn and refine your approach. Ask yourself, "What can I learn from this experience that will help me grow?"

Release Attachment to Outcomes

- While it's essential to set goals, being overly attached to specific outcomes can create stress and frustration. Focus on the actions within your control, and trust that results will come in due time. Use affirmations like, "I trust that wealth flows to me in the right way and time."

Create a Supportive Environment

- Surround yourself with people and resources that support your wealth journey. Consider joining financial communities, connecting with like-minded individuals, or reading books and materials that inspire and educate you.

EXAMPLE WEALTH PATH ROUTINE SUMMARY

Here's a sample routine that combines daily, weekly, monthly, and seasonal practices into a comprehensive, sustainable plan for wealth alignment:

Daily:

- **Morning**: Set an intention for wealth and recite a word-spell or affirmation.
- **Midday**: Take a moment to reaffirm your goals or visualise wealth.
- **Evening**: Reflect on financial experiences and express gratitude.

Weekly:

- Perform a wealth ritual, such as the Golden Path Candle Ritual, to focus your intentions for the week.
- Clear any negative energy around finances with smudging or journaling.

Monthly:

- Use the New Moon to set intentions for the month and the Full Moon to express gratitude for progress.

Seasonally:

- Set significant wealth goals at the Spring Equinox, reflect and adjust your goals at the Autumn Equinox, and celebrate financial growth at the Summer Solstice.

CREATING AN ALIGNED AND MEANINGFUL WEALTH PATH

Creating a personalised wealth path is about more than following routines; it's about cultivating a deep alignment with abundance that enhances your life. By combining intention, consistency, and self-reflection, you'll foster an enduring relationship with wealth that grows with you.

Take time to celebrate your journey, honor your achievements, and trust in your unique path to prosperity. As you integrate these practices and watch your progress unfold, you'll see how each small step builds toward a life of lasting financial abundance.

Your personalised wealth path is a dynamic, evolving journey that reflects both your financial goals and your personal growth. By committing to a routine that integrates daily, weekly, monthly, and seasonal practices, you create a steady, sustainable alignment with prosperity. This path is yours to shape, refine, and expand as you continue to grow, setting the foundation for a life of enduring wealth and abundance.

FINAL THOUGHTS

As you reach the end of this book, remember that wealth alchemy is more than a collection of rituals, practices, or techniques—it's a journey of personal transformation, one that merges the power of ancient wisdom with the intentions you bring to each day.

Through the steps you've taken, you've explored your beliefs, cultivated new habits, and opened yourself to the flow of prosperity. This journey doesn't end here; rather, it evolves with you, adapting and expanding as you continue to grow.

By aligning with wealth, you are engaging in the same timeless practices employed by some of the world's greatest minds. Like Tesla, Newton, and da Vinci, you are exploring a path that harmonises energy, thought, and action.

This alignment isn't merely about financial gain; it's about experiencing life with a deep-rooted sense of abundance in all aspects. The rituals and word-spells, combined with daily and seasonal practices, help you cultivate a wealth mindset that transcends material boundaries, bringing richness to your relationships, health, and overall well-being.

Each time you set an intention, perform a ritual, or align with the cycles of nature, you're reinforcing your connection to the energies that create abundance. Be patient with this process, and trust in the power of consistency. True alchemy is gradual, a series of small but significant shifts that, over time, reveal the transformation you seek.

As you move forward, remember that this book is a guide, but you are the creator. Feel free to adapt the practices, add your own insights, and discover what resonates most with you. Wealth alchemy is a deeply personal journey, one that honors your unique path and potential.

In closing, I encourage you to stay curious, remain open, and nurture the energy of abundance within yourself. The journey you've begun here is only the beginning.

Continue to explore, align, and attract the wealth you desire—not just in terms of money, but in the richest, fullest sense of life. Thank you for letting this book be part of your path, and may the alchemy of prosperity flourish within you.

Spooky.

www.ingramcontent.com/pod-product-compliance
Lightning Source LLC
Chambersburg PA
CBHW070128230526
45472CB00004B/1468